Making oxygen, remaining inside this pure hollow note

poems by

M. Ann Reed

Finishing Line Press
Georgetown, Kentucky

Making oxygen, remaining inside this pure hollow note

Copyright © 2020 by M Ann Reed
ISBN 978-1-64662-236-8 First Edition
All rights reserved under International and Pan-American Copyright Conventions.
No part of this book may be reproduced in any manner whatsoever without written permission from the publisher, except in the case of brief quotations embodied in critical articles and reviews.

ACKNOWLEDGMENTS

Thanks to the Jungian analyst and professor, Ann Ulanov, who inspired all of us to make oxygen in our various ways and to the editors who made room in their hearts and publications for the following poems:

Dream of making oxygen, *64 Best Poets of 2018, Halcyone-Black Mountain Press (September 2019).*
Calligraphing imagination, the historic *Red Door Literary Journal of Trinity Episcopal Cathedral, Portland, OR* (2013). Where green begins daisy (2012). Reading the land (2011). Rumi's guesthouse, earlier version (2011).
Van Cliburn's page-turner, *Psychological Perspectives, Volume 74* (2004) Issue 1, pp. 148-151. Journal entries, Volume 52 (2009) Issue 1, pp. 119-121. Should the rain sing, Volume 59 (2016) Issue 2, pp. 282-284.
Rainforest Ecstasy, the historic online *Elohi Gaduge Literary Journal* (2015). Reclaiming Night Persephone's Choice, 2014.
A peony leaps, *Mingled Voices,* an anthology of Proverse Hong Kong Press (2018).
Did you rise or fall from the cloud of unknowing? *Azure,* the online literary journal of *Lazuli Literary Group (2018)* and again in the print issue 3 (2019).
The Bodhisattva Avalokiteshvara, *Burningword Literary Journal* (January 2019).
Living in the room of stone, the earlier version appeared in the historic *EDGZ Literary Journal* (2010).
Fantasia on cummings' 'these children singing in stone', *Antithesis, the Literary Arts Journal of Melbourne University* (2017).
Hang on little tomato, *Eastern Iowa Review, Port Yonder Press (2018).*

Thanks to Finishing Line Press for welcoming this collection into the world. Thanks to my initial readers, Kim Stafford, Stephen Schneider, Claire Germane Nail and Robert Romanyshyn. Thanks to my supportive friends, Elizabeth Rose Goeke, Olga Aareskjold and Osa Aareskjold.

Publisher: Leah Maines
Editor: Christen Kincaid
Cover Art: M. Ann Reed
Author Photo: Osa Aareskjold
Cover Design: Elizabeth Maines McCleavy

Printed in the USA on acid-free paper.
Order online: www.finishinglinepress.com

Author inquiries and mail orders:
Finishing Line Press
P. O. Box 1626
Georgetown, Kentucky 40324

Table of Contents

Dream of making oxygen 1

Calligraphing 'imagination' in Wang Xi Zhu's Mandarin 2

Where green begins daisy 4

Van Cliburn's page turner 5

Should the rain sing 9

Sing for rain 11

Reading the land 12

Rain-forest ecstasy 13

A peony leaps 14

How leaps the heart 16

Did you rise or fall from the cloud of unknowing? 18

The Bodhisattva Avalokiteshvara 20

Journal entries 21

Living in the room of stone 24

Rumi's guesthouse 26

Fantasia on cummings' 'these children singing in stone' 28

Hang on, little tomato 30

Reclaiming Night Persephone's Choice 31

Preface

This journey of making oxygen begins with a child's dream of a child who holds an oxygen mask to support the breathing of people in striped pajamas as she leads them, one by one, underground, past the gas fumes of a concentration camp to liberty. The gas mask then morphs into what Rumi calls "a pure hollow note" or what Mary Caroline Richards calls that characteristic hollow at the center of a sprouting plant, likening it to "our growing point ... the child in man ... the eternally youthful element in all wisdom."* The growing point is also that through which we breathe soul-life into words, words into musical patterns, musical patterns into images, all literary features into meaning. May you enjoy this journey of making oxygen with me.

---

*See Mary Caroline Richards, *The Crossing Point*.

Dream of making oxygen

Light of no height, dark of no depth shrouds her face.
Striped pajamas cover winter's bodies.
Song of no voice deafens the silence,
music of no measure disheartens the piano—
all bewilder the speechless child
who feels none are where they belong.

No story tells the child where they belong,
no fond memory glows from the tall one's face
to remind her of her Madonna days
or to cheer these persons of clay bodies
or to tune the despondent upright piano
or to assuage this crucible of silence.

She has never tasted such ungracious silence—
this child who is not where she belongs,
who has long longed to play piano,
who fears the gaunt one's tear-eyed face,
who has never known these dry clay bodies.
Who is that one cocooned in numbness—that other child?

Yes says the oxygen mask held by the child.
Lead one by one, carefully by silence,
past these estranged, nearly blind bodies,
past barriers to the place they belong
through the passage below the harrowed face—
yes, the underground door is through the piano!

How gently the silent black and white piano
keys float dream-song over the curious child
who guides her first pilgrim toward mourning's face—
both hand-in-hand prisoners of despair's silence
who crawl beneath the keyboard toward where they belong
never forgetting behind them the forlorn bodies.

One by one diminishes the count of bodies
each heartened by keys of upright piano
and dark tunnel-winged-crawl to where they belong
oxygenated beyond lethal gas by the child
who forbears not knowing and silence
finally to see Mary's sculpted face—

face of silence, Madonna of death camps,
of new *via dolorosa* doors to where
bodies, piano, keys, and child belong.

Calligraphing imagination in Wang Xi Zhu's Mandarin

> *Days full of wanting. Let them go by . . . / Stay where you are /
> inside such a pure, hollow note.* —Rumi

1

light the pearl drop candle, hollow
   where the sand-grain
      had inspired it,

hollow
   except watery flame answering
      the wind

observe eight dimensions unfurl—
   ribbons
      of black ink

feel invisible light travel
   through the heart
      to gesturing hand

can you remain
   inside this pure
      hollow note?

2

one could say
   a black petal
      falls

curling
   toward the heart
      of light

one closed heart inclines—
   bows to imagination's opening
      heart

between two hearts braced
   apart like two harp wings
      of a grand piano

the clear page
   your heart is
      stands upright singing

a devoted love brings
   contentment
      to the heart

if there is no faithful heart,
   there is no beauty,
      no wisdom, no fascination*

sound flows
   below the ground plane touching
      water

sending up
   a black petal
      a bird returning

3

one could say ribbons of black ink migrate—
   butterflies following
      wind-days full of wanting

see them climb
   unencumbered
      to mountain summit**

feel air
   frigid in sunlight
      cool—

purify
   the burning pages
      of their wings

until they descend
   wild blue shadows inhabiting
      pure hollow notes

---

*From Handel's *Bel Piacere*.
**Every June the black butterflies migrate east, 'climbing' Mt. Hood, Oregon.

Where green begins the daisy*

> ... the sprout ... has a characteristic hollow at its center ... our growing point ... This is the child in man. The eternally youthful element in all wisdom. —Mary C. Richards, *The Crossing Point*

maybe all poems are secrets like daisies
lines—petals—seem to contradict each other
she loves me she loves me not she loves me
a white argument flows from a golden center

lines—petals—seem to contradict each other
a turbulent root sings the silent Wordsong
a white argument flows from a golden center
light opens the daisy moon

a turbulent root sings the silent Wordsong
will rocks cry out will humankind listen
light opens the daisy moon
shall we follow(to no conclusion)the stem

will rocks cry out will humankind listen
Love's lightning words clothe the naked sun
shall we follow(to no conclusion)the stem
at night closed petals hold the heart's dreams

Love's lightning words clothe the naked sun
Love's no conclusion forms the stem
at night closed petals hold heart's dreams
where green begins to shape white petals

Love's no conclusion forms the stem
the sun dreams of being a daisy—wonders
where green begins to shape white petals
will love touch me forever

the sun dreams of being a daisy—wonders
maybe all poems are secrets like daisies
will Love touch me forever
she loves me she loves me not she loves me
where green begins to shape white petals

---

*Linda Pastan's new verse form.

Van Cliburn's page-turner

> *After the waves have told their story . . . / they sound their note . . .*
> —Kim Stafford, *Wind on the Waves*

She sings a way
   through night of heart,
      through dark, dreamless sleep,

learning
   where ultraviolet
      tone poems begin,

where light
   like a medicine wheel
      travels

playing harmony
   before suffering
      into colors.

There in this birthplace
   she meets
      the sacred musician

who suffers
   colors' return
      to white light.

This time,
   he is Van Cliburn,
      and she is his page turner.

They dream
   their dreaming
      the center of a rose,

a chambered
   nautilus
      rose.

This rose dreams them too,
   seats them upon
      an ebony piano bench

where they hover,
   attending the sea,
      their bodies

phosphorescing
   Titian red and gold,
      their faces

turning amber.
   Have the waves told you
      their story?

Like wind-fingers flowing
   through ivory
      petals

his fingers bend
   to pure
      silent Word.

Waves join
   their listening,
      break open ocean's

glass door,
   and they follow
      the promising

white horse
   with wings,
      follow roller coaster

crescendos
   of black-winged
      birds becoming

shadows of their flight—
   shadows
      mechanical encrusted

upon a page, shedding
   bodies of light.
      Wind blows, turns

crisp white pages,
   water wings clapping
      a thousand white

butterflies pealing
   forth,
      somersaulting

their white frenzy,
   dancing
      iridescent waves,

each kaleidoscopic
   spun glass.
      Each intricate

interwoven wing
   brings them home,
      liquid

light bodies enfolded
   in Paschal
      flame.

Have the waves
   told their story?
      No, their story is

too painful
   to tell.
      Not reading the score

but the music,
   wave upon wave
      of sorrow

poured out—
   Rosh Hashana song
      climbing the rocks—

we pray
   for music to shatter,
      remake us

alone,
   amourtized
      into time is not.

She tells him
    her mother is
        Cosmos

divinely ordered,
    her father is
        Creative Chaos.

She is Honeyhum,
    Dreamwalker.
        Her best friends

are Tao Bear
    and Wished-for-Sister,
        Sacred

Empty Space,
    Unborn Moment,
        Plumblossom,

Full-of-New-Life.
    He names her Soul-Bride,
        Butterfly

Woman,
    Sacred Interpreter.
        She names

him Water-through-Wine,
    Wildness-
        of-Innisfree.

Together they name
    the ocean
        Islands-

of-Glass,
    Undertow-of-Dolphins,
        A Fine Madness Retained.*

---

*Michael Drayton (1563-1631) offered this tribute to Christopher Marlowe.

Should the rain sing

> *To live is so startling it leaves little time / for anything else.*
> —Emily Dickinson

Reading Emily, dying
   for Beauty through songs
      of lightning, brings

Lady Death to her feet.
   Her skeleton, absolving white, fascinates—troubles
      the night.

Her living bones are light.
   From Her backbone unfurls
      a feather—ribs or wings?

From Her shoulders She feels—knows how to fly.
   Wait, She intimates, *listen,*
      should the rain sing.

At high noon, She is
   breathless alive with flocks
      of yellow finch, testing

cherry branch,
   Japanese bridal veil,
      and white-lime summer snowball.

At midnight, She is
   and is not.
      She feels alone,

though in the company of stars.
   She communes
      with branches of pine bent

low by green moustaches and
   wizardly goatees.
      She feels at home with

each also alone
   branch separated
      from what it touches,

    yet inseparable
        from the stars.
            With the pink Yves Piaget

Rose of sun,
    She opens inside each
        parabola of birch.

When the heart ceases to beat
    as fascination's electricity flows
        through it—*pauses*

in ecstasy
    as Galvani had described—
        inspired imagination beholds

Lady Death enchanting
    us across eccentricity's thresholds,
        into worlds of love and delight.

Had Emily known Her as I know Her?
    A keen lightning into keener life?
        I wait,

listen, should the rain sing.
    How do we know Spirit
        from Dust?

Sing for rain—

there is nothing softer
claims Lao Tsu,
there is nothing more
incisive.

Like crystal shards,
like wings of broken glass,
wind-driven rain stings
my skin

      I am porous earth,
the horse Eucalyptus running wild,
Rain Dancer bonding
to Light Spirit's Wind,
ground lightning's song piercing
tumbling charcoal clouds,

and as rain rounds
to clarity—bonds
with winter's wisteria
to bead her barren branches—
our hearts of wood bond—soften
into the one black
character gravid
with Buddha.

Reading the land

on a gradual grade
    I-10 passes over high chaparral country;
in tandem the soul crescendos
    incrementally to high C

red rocks appear
    like red men commanding
a completely enchanted silence directing
    inner and outer scene

are they masked dancers
    personas wind(whimsically) tossed together
or immortals—
    Taoists speaking—breathed
like children become shy
    into this drama of one tribe

    through their strong bodies
sage brush peer
    Texas Mountain Laurel and Desert willow spiral
their wind-bent s-curves bowing
    to honor the One Breath
exhaling this garden
    this red rock
this One Song singing us into being
    singing this place where we may be
(as we once were) surprised
    into trees*

---

*Inspired by Nancy Wood's *Spirit Walker*.

Rain-forest ecstasy
   radiating to Pacific ocean and Antarctic climes

tangerine monkeys   spring   on ancient banana feet

                    applaud(dash)ing
                         ecstatic
                         starCries
                                              announcing
                                              trap(ezery)
               Hummingbirdtelegrams twist

(choose)rush of breath   a blueprint electric   of dots and dash

                                  across apricot tiger flats

           kinkajous plunge   swing
                                       on curtailing amaze

and moon-faced Night Monkey wakes   at dusk
                                    to sail the new moonship Iguana

                         hush
        dragons are fireflies   the forest ahum

plummeting
     Harpy Eagles fly
            upside(suddenly) down   and Quetzal feathers whisper

                       come hug
                the chanting edge of Dolphins
              their erotic brother wears a coat of rain

                         knows

it takes the swaddling stillness of Penguins   to keep the balance of us

            and little leaf-nosed bats track
                              ground lightning—

              wing(thunderclap)

                    upon wing

A peony leaps

> *Only with the heart one may see rightly . . . / What is essential is invisible to the eye.* —Antoine de Saint-Exupéry, The Little Prince

Paint this peony, invites Wang Gongyi.
    No, I can't.
        Yes, you can. Learn to paint from life.

The peony's infinitely unfurling
    coastline of repeating waves receding
        into tinctures of darker to darkest pink, had lost

fullest poise—
    that momentary stay
        against confusion.*

Attuning to musical coastlines, why
    does my hand refuse my eyes?
        Keep it. Look again—next year.

By morning my hand understands
    (without thought or eyes) intricately felt gestures
        of peony coastlines.**

Peony after peony quickly marries
    hand, gesture, paper, brush and ink, happy
        to live through art.

In her accordion book of hours,
    last evening's peony and children debut,
        gravid in black, charcoal, grey, pale grey and white petalage.

Yet her story remains half-told.
    On her birthday, I see what she had impressed—
        simultaneous birth, growth, maturation,

decline, death and the constellating moment
    of regeneration and rebirth—
        what plant cells teach botanists peering

through high-powered electron-microscopes—
    what botanist-poet Emily Dickinson directly knew
        and understood.

---

*From Robert Frost's "Directive."
**Chinese call such a gift of transmission from the life force *Wu Wei* or 'effortlessness.'

Muse of mystery, icon of life force,
    this peony had transmitted
        from her deep reveries

a force of increasing potentials told
    by each wave of coastline (hidden from dying
        thoughts and eyes) born of Dream.

How leaps the heart?

a reflection on St. Julian's revelations, part 1

Rain
silver transit of my joy sings crescent
the new moon

Foot upon wave
(sapphire respondent
to a voice) we are
steady as we go
deep into our
impossible blue
of rose.

There is no return to the boat.

There is no question (cane pole bent brooding
over green water quiet with hope) no
question of walking on water dreaming
water, wonder and flora-fauna-fish,
no question of fishing but wonder perched
orange like the straw coolie on my head, orange
wonder puffing into jacket the orange
of life singing *There's a rainbow 'round
my shoulder* pulling down deep into the green
quiet of water and fish, no question
it would be no small catch, no small fish luring
out the dory (green, wooden) into the thick
of lake to wait green with still trees dropping
impatience into hope to bob orange, white
and fragile with dreams; no, there is no estrangement
between me and the sparks electric—

fiery with fourth of July fish, gold
nuggets of true self, hiding deep
in the gentle of hope, no estrangement
between me and the shore of sandy beach
and fossils cuniforming the deep
and trees hieroglyphing the up
of sun; no, there is no question
of disconnection, no question of dream
apart from dreamer, no question
of joyful leap to separate
sunfish from fisher in the sun

               there is only the wide

    separate   question
                            why?

**Did you rise or fall from
    the cloud of unknowing?**

A spark of divine inspiration?
    A phoenix-flame inside drops of rain?

    Rain sings tonight.
    Each drop holds a pear-shaped flame.
    Paradrops fall to form fluent silk screens.

Did someone's dying breath gift you
    to inherit the memory of Keats,
one day to write your name in water
    to gift another poet your breath?

    You are more than blood—birth in a bowl.
    You breathe holy secrets.
    Pears fall from the sky.

Did you choose your parents?
    (Or did they call you? Learn to sing your song?)
Were you present when Yahweh banished Gaia from divine grace
    to subjugate women and nature to the will of men?

    Fire and water marry their differences.

Or have you always lived when Gan Eden thrived—
    a garden enlivened by diversity and friendship?
Lived in that dwelling well kept from any *where*,
    ever in the *when* of all times

    Rain and song leaf out.

Did you follow Socrates through Athens, learning to unravel
    with a question all the reasons that oppress life?
When did we try to kill you?
    And in killing you, kill our selves?

    Paradrops fall.

At sunrise, you are the giant peach surrounding
    the rough ruby pit of you.
At sunset, you are the beating ruby pit, relinquishing
    the juicy peach.

    You are a paradox.

And what do you say to the five hundred millions of stars?
    That seventy million old cells die as we sleep
and seventy million new cells are born?
    That we perpetually evolve, so best not judge?

A Chambered Nautilus Madonna holds you,
Her Child, a lit candle in the Whirlpool Galaxy

The Bodhisattva Avalokiteshvara

> *"What caravan did the Thousand Oaks shooter [terrorist] come from?"*
> —*Don Lemon*

Recent news ended, *Terrorists suspected.*
    Among the frenzied crowd cued
        in Harvest Bakery's lunch line,
            a mother's quietude commands.

Her shoulder-length brown hair frames a smooth ivory-skinned face;
    her brown silk raincoat nearly camouflages
        her severed left arm carried
            invisible like the dead.

Like the seen-unseen homeless.
    Like the increasing refugees who,
        after journalists air their plights, disappear fractured
            by the next featured frame.

Faces press upon clay memory—
    embed the snapdragon-black eyes
        like those of this mother's adopted
            Ethiopian daughter who peers

from behind the silk rain of her mother's coat—peers
    from her perfectly proportioned Nefertiti face.
        Peers have taunted her—have demonized
            her alleged illegitimacy, yet her mother's *got sand*—

Huck Finn's words spoken
    of Mary Jane, kind to all strangers
        (kind to all of us new in every moment.)
        She has let go.

With invisible arm she marries the dead, the disenfranchised,
    the migrants, unseen witnesses.
        Never choosing between keeping neighbors
            or adopting daughters, she says yes to her love-life.

        Hugging that *yes* her child tugs the sleeve hiding
        the map of woe bound for imperfect paradise.

Journal entries

    1.

the full moon door
    transparent amber
        climbs

Mt. Hood
    a white linen
        on gloaming's French blue

absolutely
    nothing is
        impossible

    2.

the Lake Superior stone
    angular
        buff-colored

bears
    the uncanny cameo
        of my mother

so far
    the resemblance eludes
        all but me

i point
    to the nineteen
        thirty-one black

and white
    engagement photo
        this is my mother

notice how
    the left eyelid droops
        how lips smiling

over teeth draw
    a wave
        i point

to the Lake Superior
   cameo
      this is

my mother
   notice how
      the left eyelid droops

how lips smiling
   over teeth draw
      a wave

i watch
   the blind become
      bewildered

then realize
   the stone
      had not chosen them

absolutely
   nothing happens
      by chance

   3.

the child Paul
   opens the book
      Raven's New Adventures

he creates
   his theatre
      of the invisible

lifts
   holds out
      his chair

defends himself
   tames
      a roaring lion

truth-telling
   holds captive
      his imagination

we entertain
   true questions
      real routes

scientists could travel
   Paul is
      a little prince

who reminds
   us never to let go
      of a question

   4.

the green karmic door
   hinges
      upon *ripe-etude*

composes
   Asian pears
      full of summer sun

pleases palates
   in salads
      or globe-fruited eyes

asks
   are you ripening
      too

Living in the room of stone

a letter to Dr. Zaki, Cairo, Egypt:

Do you live where voices silenced are bones
buried within you?* Where generations decompose,
their fine dust recomposing, teaching you

not to accept only what is helpful
and to discard the rest? Even in this practice,
this swan-medicine of surrender,

do you feel the blessing elude you?
Do the oaks of Mamre at Hebron seem
to diminish? Does Abraham's altar appear

archaic, a mere artifact when you hear
the new scientific question, *What is
the difference between carbon and silicon life?*

You search heaven, numbering the stars.
There the loops of your father's Arabic letters find
you tracing your people's poetry in the sky.

Each star is a flaming eye, a Seraph's pulse guarding
your soul's house, the patient in your care.
Tomorrow you will poem a heart surgery.

You do not ask who is patient, who is surgeon.
Each of you bears the same cardiac disease.
Perhaps your patient will hold steady your hand,

while you remind him of a spiraling plan.
He is the starfire, the treasure between
heaven and earth. You both will become one

heartmind, your hands dreaming the golden door
of moon, restoring the life-is-round vibration.
You ponder your art of closure, the surgeon's poetics

of leaving scars, grief's letters etched into flesh.
You wonder how you and your patient will be
stronger in the mended places, wonder if

---

*Echo from Naomi Shihab Nye's "Biography of an Armenian School Girl."

the loops of your father's letters now threading
your poem will suture wings of light.
Cairo disappears, that place where you labor in love,

where you make time, almost in your sleep,
to memorize each patient, each quirk and quark,
each one's numbered days and yours.

They all survive, and so do you. All play
in your dreams, mingling with your midnight research,
your dawn's vocation to pray.

You count patients in constellations of three.
Three is all i can give my best care.
In your mind, one is always Jewish,

the second Muslim, the third Christian.
Though war increases the dead, you wait
for brown grass full of verdant ferns unfurling

roses of lavender light. Tomorrow
you will weave your poem into the map
of your patient's body, incarnating

a new vital sign, making smooth
the rough disharmonies, changing
the boundaries of our lives.

Rumi's guesthouse, Mostar, Bosnia-Herzegovina

Ancient stones had received the bullets, ejected
        hostile guests. Still
(mason's lace rudely interrupted, kindly intact)
        foundation and framework hold true—accept
the redolent arms they had once restricted—accept
        earth's green embrace.
Imaginations trace
        new limits,   new extents
why not let the roof be the sky
        the rooms be more spacious—leave
windows and doors uncapped
        a few hinges for
                Wings!
                All God's chill'un
                got t' have
wings,*
    dithyrambic struck strings,
        comings and goings

of fluttering things,
    ringed chrystograph
        of tree,
harp,
    piano.
        Fine-tuned pings of long-stemmed

crystalline,
    imagined doors swinging
        from chrysamine,

all measure
    Bidondo's
        morning praise—

billowing reverie
    of flowing
        water,

chrystocrene
    shoulder blades
        of blue mountains,

---

*Echoes Eugene O'Neill's title of a dramatic work.

graveling,
    travelling grumbles
        of bee-loud

bossa novas,
    marigold petals
        of corn-chrysanthemums, all toll

us back
    to ourselves.
        We are human,

not made of stone
    but fragile flesh
        and bone

challenged to grow
    more supple,
        more nimble-minded and humane.

Fantasia on cummings' 'these children singing in stone'

Poems are born from infancy. —Seamus Heaney

If the dreamer, Ernest's stonewall begins
    a bundle of fragments, is it because
        his hands know particle, wave and wavicle—know

all particles are one? As he receives each stone, one by one,
    is it because he is memorizing earth's art
        deeply within or because he knows each

punctuated equilibria—each birthplace
    in the fossil record by the palms of his heart?
        As Ernest sculpts a collage of earth's carvings,

is it because his hands belong to an undefined,
    unbound mystery? Or to the broken open word?
        Should the collage suggest the bee-hive's hexagonal

lattice-work and the turtle's octagonal shell,
    is it because Ernest is composing the stones' song
        of six-eight time? If he lacks lyrics for this song,

is it because he remembers *good fences make*
    good neighbors? Or because he wonders if his hands
        imitate something old and outworn or improvise

something new and unpredictable? When,
    on his birthday, February fourteenth,
        Ernest Valentine pauses from his labour,

is it to ponder the number of his days?
    Or to begin a new ritual —begin
        to send his niece a box of chocolates,

a mosaic with each morsel arranged
    curiously like a stonewall? Is he finding
        delicious the vanishing points? His disappearing acts?

The new possibilities? *Shall I fine-tune the wall*
    or me? ... Yet already the stones have revised him,
        transmitting their desire to sound *hyvrid (lovely)*—

that encouraging, hovering bird of a Welsh word born
    of listening. If Ernest continues to quilt
        granite and quartz, is it because he feels

the sounds omitted weigh less than the silence salvaged?
   Or because, like the wall, he listens to a silent film?
      Continuing his art, Ernest recalls

the Edwardian boy he was, wearing a blue dress,
    the boy who knew that (not fences but) self-forgetting
      beauty makes good neighbours. If Ernest no longer sits

by his wall, is it because he refuses
   to regard his failures? Or because the porous
     solidity of strength, beauty and listening

has become a song he hears everywhere?
   Or is it because in the everywhere silence
      of his childhood, he still sings of a stillness

more still than a
   lit tle
   tree listens
   forever to always children singing forever
   a song made
   of silent as stone silence of
   song*

---

*ADAPTED from "these children singing in stone a". Copyright 1939, © 1967, 1991 by the Trustees for the E. E. Cummings Trust, from *COMPLETE POEMS: 1904-1962* by E. E. Cummings, edited George J. Firmage. Used by permission of Liveright Publishing Corporation.

Hang on, little tomato

for Lydia

I *am six, five, four, three, two, one going on one-hundred-thousand years old. Every day is a birthday. So the dates on the new gravestone, 1928—2015, confuse me.* I read the credits: Minoan Sisterhood Founder, Traveler, Artist, Mystic, Human-i-tar-ian *(another dinosaur?)* Epi-curean (from 'cure'? a physician?) Culinary Artist, Social Activist for Peace, Women's Rights, Caring Economics, and Cultural Trans-form- a-tion. *What are my credits? I am gullible. I am a crisis. (Everyone laughed with me when I used these new words in sentences— even my teacher who said I am getting to know myself. That Socrates would be proud of me.) A photographer pauses 'perplexed' (my new word). Like she may or may not snap my picture. She studies me—makes me aware that I am still in my black leotard and pink tutu—that my black hair hangs wild and loose past my shoulders—that ballet class was 'rigorous' (my favorite new word)—that my energy is stronger. My ballet teacher notices that I sit like a Tai Chi Master, legs in wide, open second position, feet firmly planted like the pine tree. When I sit like that, I feel more open-minded, yet kind of vulnerable. I am still only four feet, three inches tall. My height on the library reading scale still places me in the primary reading group. When I reach my arm high over my head, my height is way beyond the top reading level. Then I feel almost the way I did when I met a bear at Yellowstone this summer: terrified, exhilarated.*

Reclaiming Night Persephone's choice

> *Every thirst gets satisfied except / that of these fish, the mystics, / who swim a vast ocean of grace / still somehow longing for it!* —Rumi

1

around coral reefs, Night swims
gravid
with zebras,
angels, betas and
Persephone.

        toward whom
        does she swim
        trailing arms of phosphorescing
        fish?

a mandala,
a voice of eye radiates
moon.

        whose voices
        heavy with sand call
        her?

2

there he lay
impressing
one simple circle
upon the fossil
memory

        there he lay
        precisely where he had fallen
        his wax wings
         cooled and curled
        intact
        about his mute body—
        Icarus whose splash
        of creative spark passed

disregarded
by all except
his sensitive father

        the architect
        Daedalus

who like Brueghel

        had known
        the world
        of callous men

yet who could not (like Brueghel) paint
the son's fall
a background event
to the year

        Spring
        waking up
        alacritous

when farmers plough
their fields
when

        melting
        wings are

insignificant

who could not (like William Carlos Williams
and Auden who had known
the world made by industrial revolutionists) paint
the scene an unnoticed splash—

        Daedalus, under Cummings' wing, erased
        the failed poetic act—found
        Icarus an angel burning from
        generous completely light learning
        the depths of horror to defend
        a sunbeam's architecture with his life*

His despair
his humiliation congeals, recording
the world's contempt
for vulnerability

---

*XXII, *E. E. Cummings' Complete Poems 1913-1962*, p. 562.

his jaw fixes
the rosinized stare
transparent
green from nibbling
crayfish

3

   she lay
   almost invisible
   beside him

   radiant
   animated

Andromeda
whose head still rests
on the very navel

   the rose
   of Pegasus

4

   what forgotten words
   could guide
   these two
   could direct
   them up from
   their watery grave

what did you learn Icarus?
what did you teach me?

   look up Icarus
   your eccentric wax
   wing experiments
   have made you well
   you no longer need them
   accept your creative gift

   and fly
   fly with the genius
   who gives you life

*and what
Andromeda
did you learn*

*that the world deceives
that you are
off the map?*

what did you teach me?

> *accept the holiness
> of your heart's affections
> return to disarm
> the certain world
> with life's germinating
> mystery*

5

one day
      one Life
one leaftime
      uncertain
two awoke
      remembering

someOne died

      two someOnes were born**

**Echo of Li Young Lee's "My Father's House" from *Book of My Nights*.

www.ingramcontent.com/pod-product-compliance
Lightning Source LLC
LaVergne TN
LVHW041559070426
835507LV00011B/1183